Name

Date

To parents If possible, have your child write his or her name in the box above. On this page, your child will connect the first five uppercase letters of the alphabet. From this page on, the number of letters will gradually increase. Please have your child say the letters aloud while he or she is tracing.

■ While saying each letter aloud, draw a line from Ⓐ to Ⓔ to connect the letters in alphabetical order.

| A | B | C | D | E |

■ While saying each letter aloud, draw a line from Ⓐ to Ⓔ to connect the letters in alphabetical order.

| A | B | C | D | E |

Uppercase Letters
Saying **A** → **J**

■ While saying each letter aloud, draw a line from Ⓐ to Ⓙ to connect the letters in alphabetical order.

| A | B | C | D | E | F | G | H | I | J |

■ While saying each letter aloud, draw a line from Ⓐ to Ⓙ to connect the letters in alphabetical order.

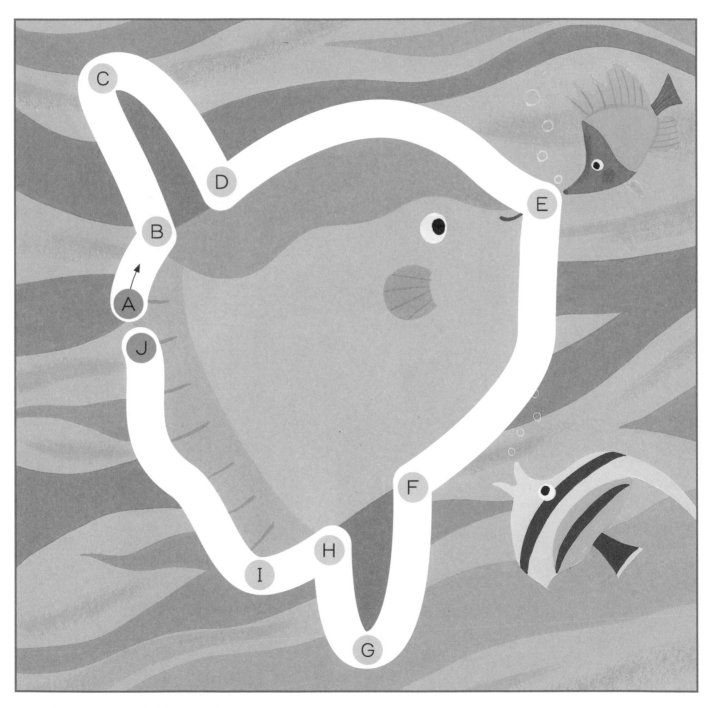

| A | B | C | D | E | F | G | H | I | J |

■ While saying each letter aloud, draw a line from Ⓐ to Ⓞ to connect the letters in alphabetical order.

| A | B | C | D | E | F | G | H | I | J | K | L | M | N | O |

■ While saying each letter aloud, draw a line from Ⓐ to Ⓞ to connect the letters in alphabetical order.

| A | B | C | D | E | F | G | H | I | J | K | L | M | N | O |

■ While saying each letter aloud, draw a line from Ⓐ to Ⓣ to connect the letters in alphabetical order.

| A | B | C | D | E | F | G | H | I | J | K | L | M | N | O | P | Q | R | S | T |

■ While saying each letter aloud, draw a line from Ⓐ to Ⓣ to connect the letters in alphabetical order.

| A | B | C | D | E | F | G | H | I | J | K | L | M | N | O | P | Q | R | S | T |

■ While saying each letter aloud, draw a line from Ⓐ to Ⓩ to connect the letters in alphabetical order.

| A | B | C | D | E | F | G | H | I | J | K | L | M | N | O | P | Q | R | S | T | U | V | W | X | Y | Z |

■ While saying each letter aloud, draw a line from Ⓐ to Ⓩ to connect the letters in alphabetical order.

| A | B | C | D | E | F | G | H | I | J | K | L | M | N | O | P | Q | R | S | T | U | V | W | X | Y | Z |

10

Uppercase Letters
Writing **A** and **B**

Name

....

Date

To parents Before your child begins writing, please read the words on the page and ask your child to repeat them after you. If your child can recognize the letters, try having him or her tell you the name of each letter. In any case, please help your child say the name of the letter and its sound as he or she is tracing.

■ Trace the letters.

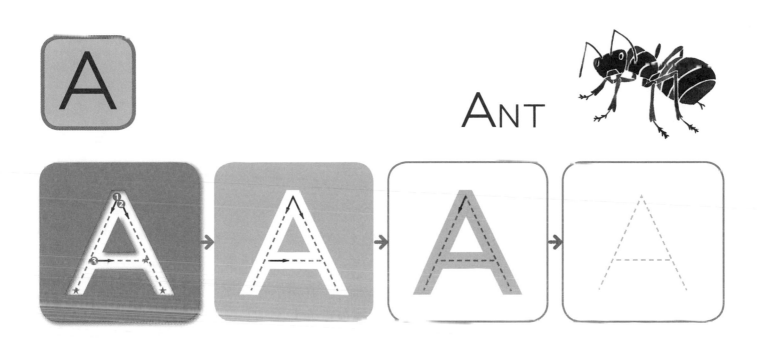

Aɴᴛ

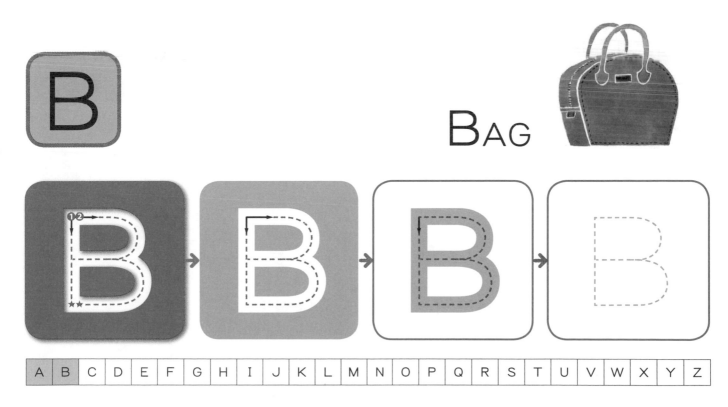

Bᴀɢ

| A | B | C | D | E | F | G | H | I | J | K | L | M | N | O | P | Q | R | S | T | U | V | W | X | Y | Z |

Writing **C** and **D**

■ Trace the letters.

C

CAT

D

DOG

A	B	C	D	E	F	G	H	I	J	K	L	M	N	O	P	Q	R	S	T	U	V	W	X	Y	Z

Uppercase Letters
Writing **E** and **F**

■ Trace the letters.

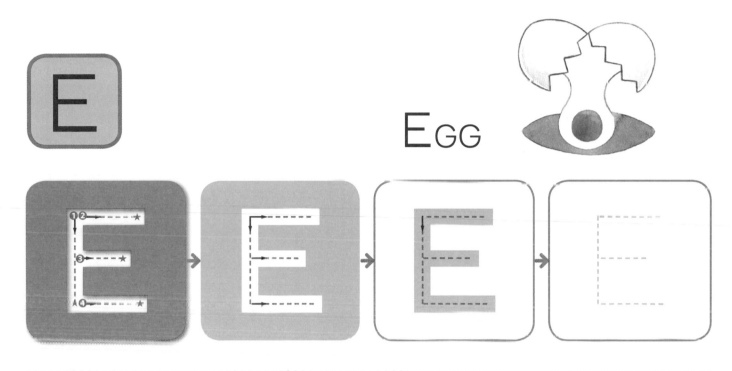

Egg

Fox

| A | B | C | D | E | F | G | H | I | J | K | L | M | N | O | P | Q | R | S | T | U | V | W | X | Y | Z |

Writing **G** and **H**

■ Trace the letters.

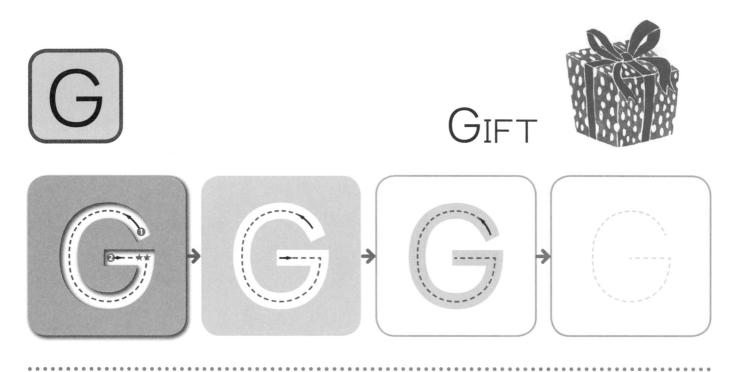

GIFT

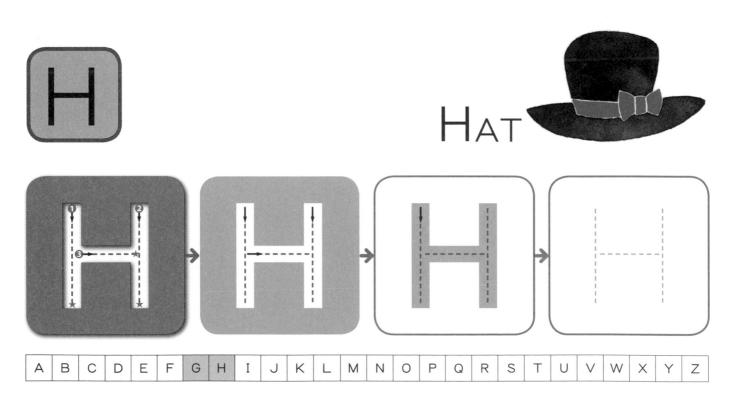

HAT

| A | B | C | D | E | F | G | H | I | J | K | L | M | N | O | P | Q | R | S | T | U | V | W | X | Y | Z |

14

To parents   If your child is having difficulty tracing any of these letters, try our other workbooks, such as *My First Book of UPPERCASE LETTERS*, for additional practice.

■ Trace the letters.

INK

JAM

| A | B | C | D | E | F | G | H | I | J | K | L | M | N | O | P | Q | R | S | T | U | V | W | X | Y | Z |

Writing **K** and **L**

■ Trace the letters.

KEY

LION

| A | B | C | D | E | F | G | H | I | J | K | L | M | N | O | P | Q | R | S | T | U | V | W | X | Y | Z |

■ Trace the letters.

M

MAT

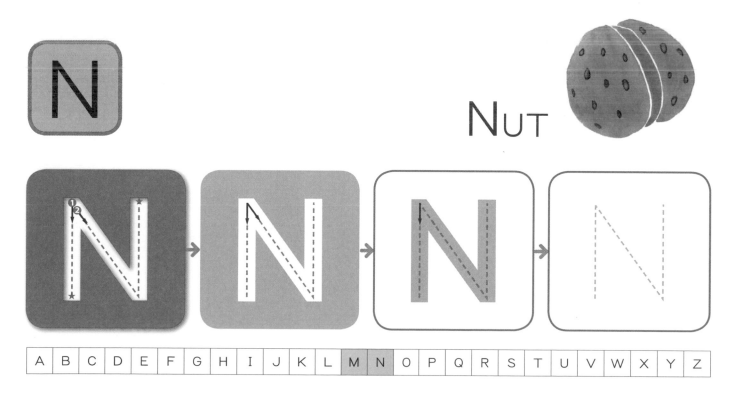

N

NUT

Writing **O** and **P**

■ Trace the letters.

ORANGE

PAN

To parents Because of the way these letters are shaped, they are particularly difficult to write. Please praise your child for their hard work.

■ Trace the letters.

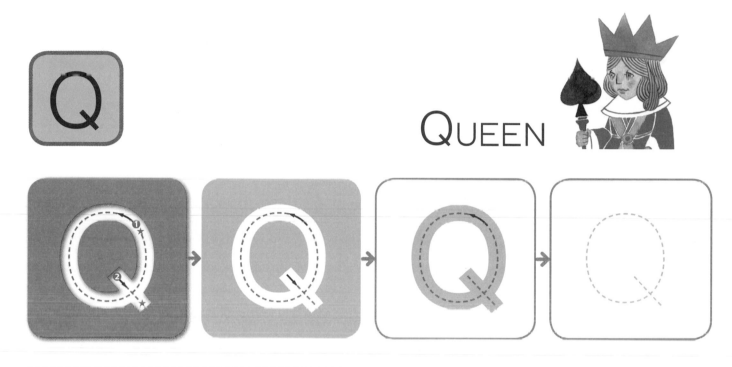

QUEEN

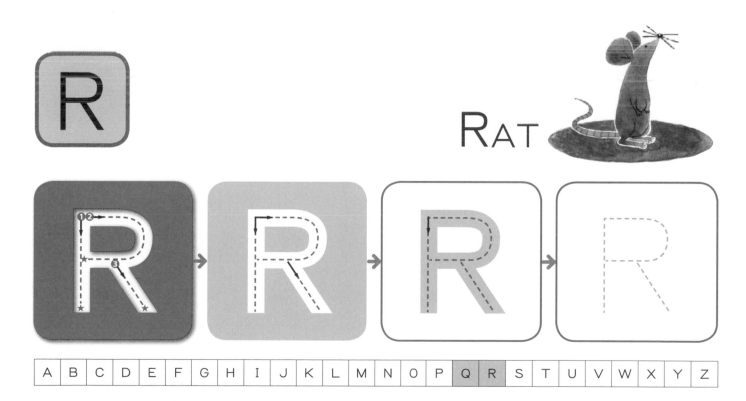

RAT

| A | B | C | D | E | F | G | H | I | J | K | L | M | N | O | P | Q | R | S | T | U | V | W | X | Y | Z |

Writing **S** and **T**

■ Trace the letters.

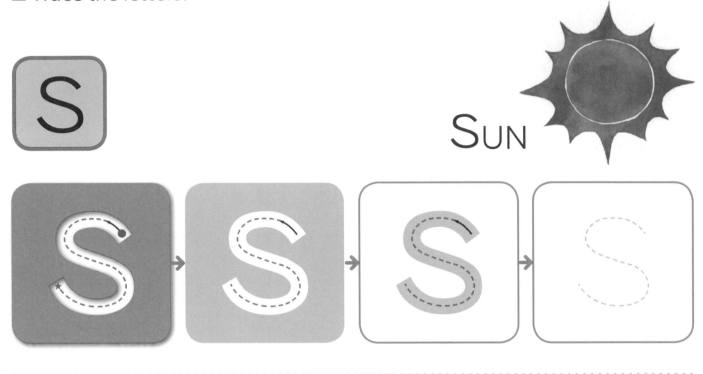

S

SUN

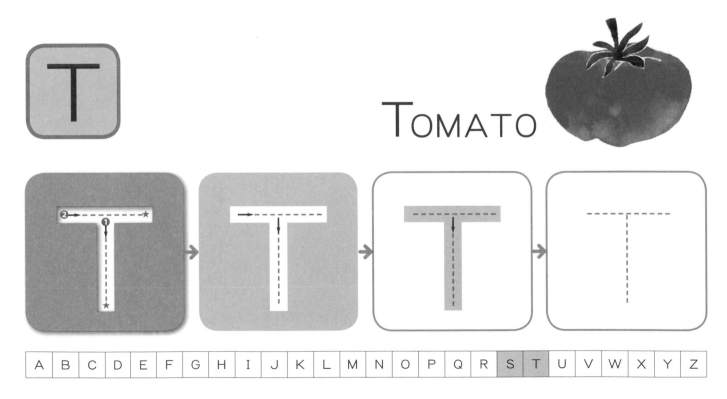

T

TOMATO

| A | B | C | D | E | F | G | H | I | J | K | L | M | N | O | P | Q | R | S | T | U | V | W | X | Y | Z |

■ Trace the letters.

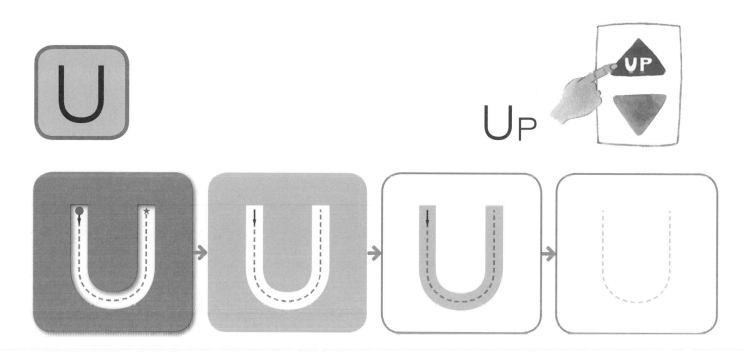

U_P

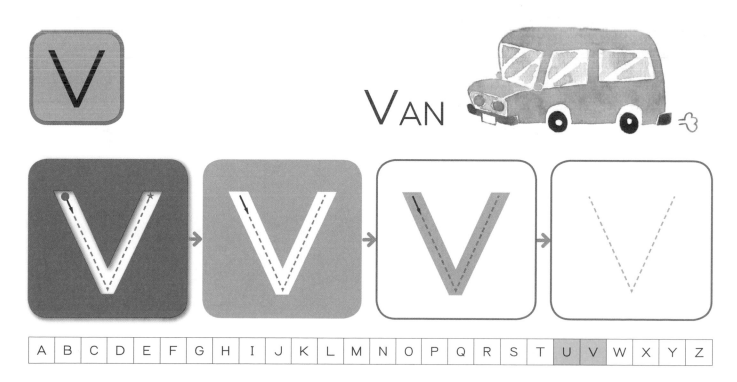

V_AN

| A | B | C | D | E | F | G | H | I | J | K | L | M | N | O | P | Q | R | S | T | U | V | W | X | Y | Z |

21

Writing **W** and **X**

■ Trace the letters.

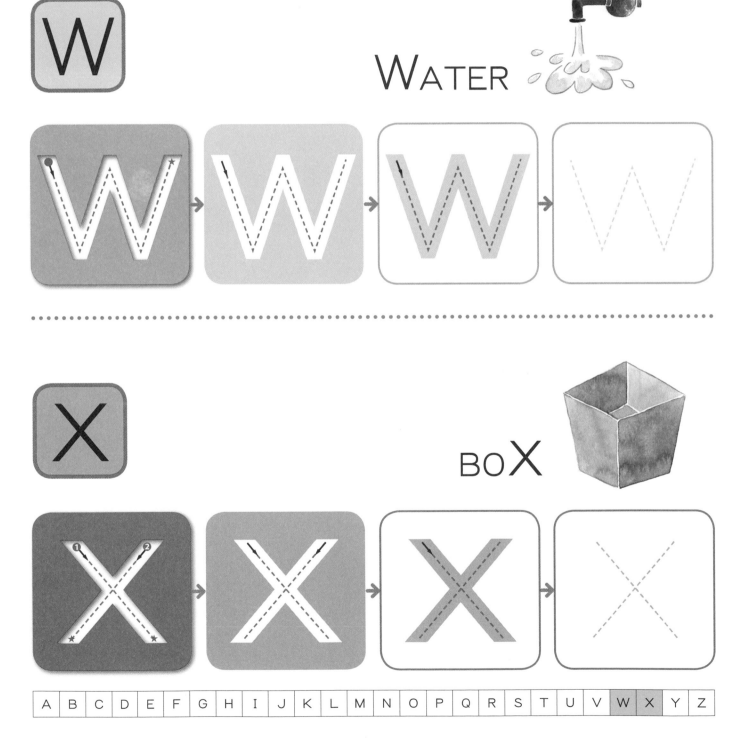

W

WATER

X

BOX

| A | B | C | D | E | F | G | H | I | J | K | L | M | N | O | P | Q | R | S | T | U | V | W | X | Y | Z |

Uppercase Letters
Writing **Y** and **Z**

Name

Date

■ Trace the letters.

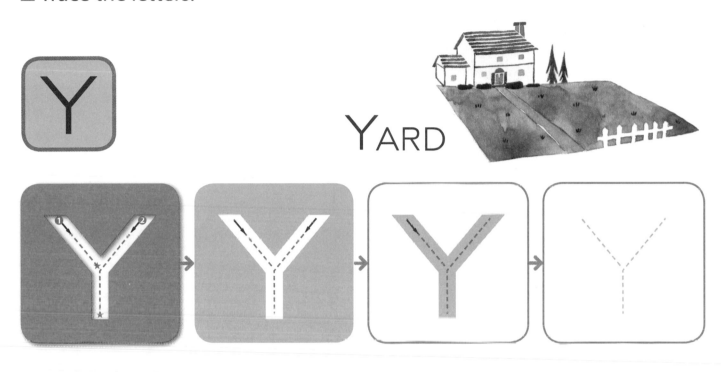

YARD

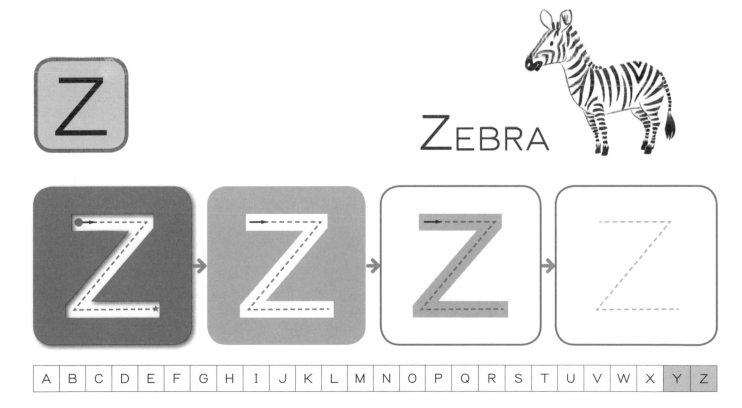

ZEBRA

| A | B | C | D | E | F | G | H | I | J | K | L | M | N | O | P | Q | R | S | T | U | V | W | X | Y | Z |

Review **A** to **Z**

■ Trace the letters in the table below.

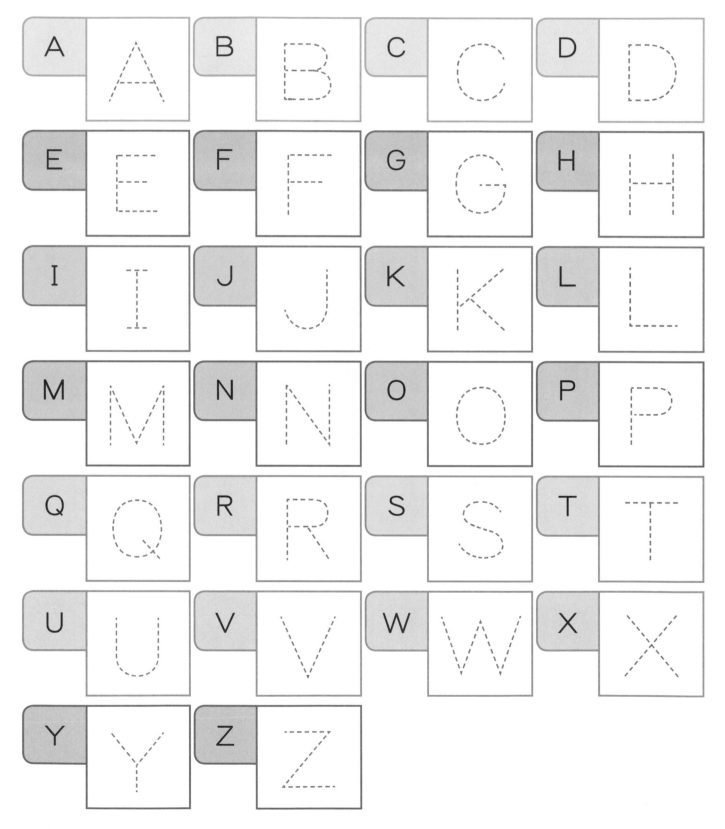

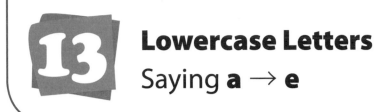

To parents On this page, your child will connect the first five letters of the lowercase alphabet. From this page on, the number of letters will gradually increase. Please have your child say the letters aloud while he or she is connecting the dots.

■ While saying each letter aloud, draw a line from a to e to connect the letters in alphabetical order.

a b c d e

(bag)

■ While saying each letter aloud, draw a line from a to e to connect the letters in alphabetical order.

a	b	c	d	e

(boat)

Lowercase Letters
Saying **a** → **j**

■ While saying each letter aloud, draw a line from a to j to connect the letters in alphabetical order.

| a | b | c | d | e | f | g | h | i | j |

27

(dog)

■ While saying each letter aloud, draw a line from a to j to connect the letters in alphabetical order.

| a | b | c | d | e | f | g | h | i | j |

(hat)

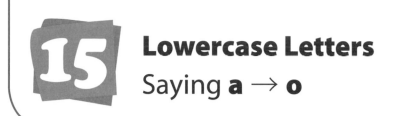

■ While saying each letter aloud, draw a line from **a** to **o** to connect the letters in alphabetical order.

| a | b | c | d | e | f | g | h | i | j | k | l | m | n | o |

(apple)

■ While saying each letter aloud, draw a line from a to o to connect the letters in alphabetical order.

a	b	c	d	e	f	g	h	i	j	k	l	m	n	o

(whale)

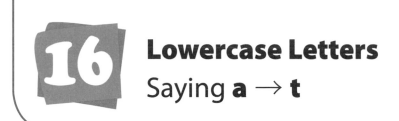
■ While saying each letter aloud, draw a line from a to t to connect the letters in alphabetical order.

| a | b | c | d | e | f | g | h | i | j | k | l | m | n | o | p | q | r | s | t |

31

(car)

■ While saying each letter aloud, draw a line from a to t to connect the letters in alphabetical order.

a	b	c	d	e	f	g	h	i	j	k	l	m	n	o	p	q	r	s	t

(elephant)

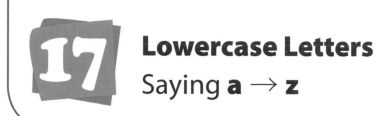

Lowercase Letters
Saying **a** → **z**

■ While saying each letter aloud, draw a line from a to z to connect the letters in alphabetical order.

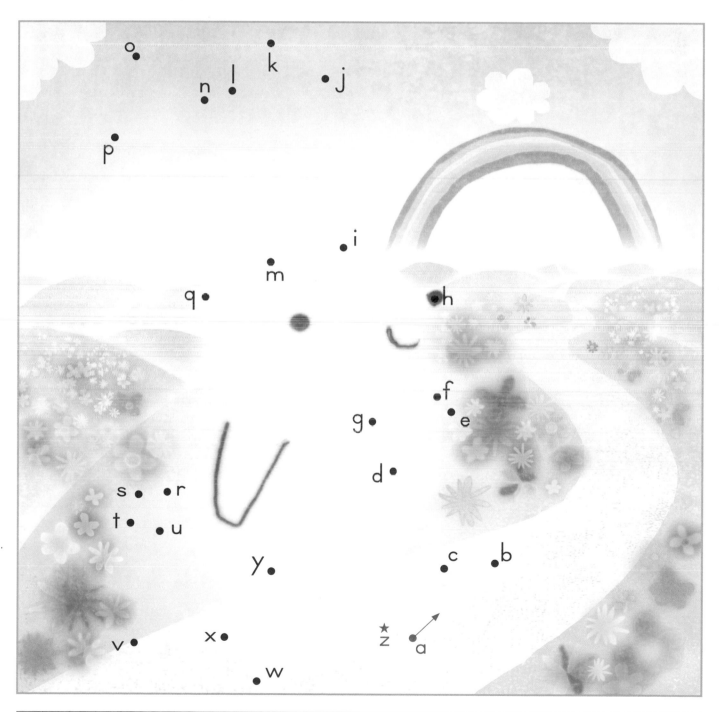

a	b	c	d	e	f	g	h	i	j	k	l	m	n	o	p	q	r	s	t	u	v	w	x	y	z

(rabbit)

■ While saying each letter aloud, draw a line from a to z to connect the letters in alphabetical order.

| a | b | c | d | e | f | g | h | i | j | k | l | m | n | o | p | q | r | s | t | u | v | w | x | y | z |

(rocket)

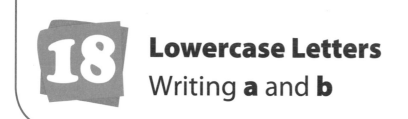

18 Lowercase Letters
Writing **a** and **b**

Name
....
Date

To parents Writing lowercase letters is even harder than writing uppercase letters. When your child completes an exercise, be sure to praise him or her.

■ Trace the letters.

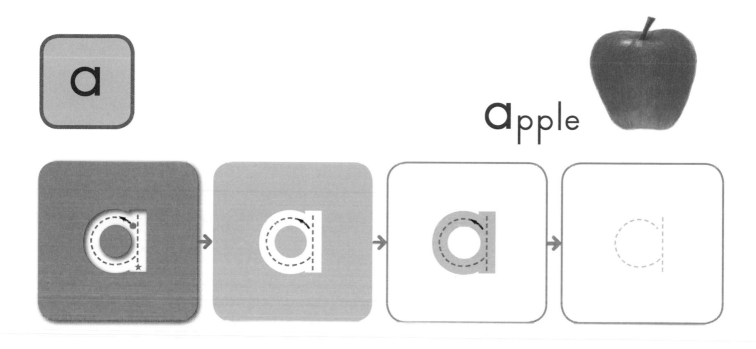

a
apple

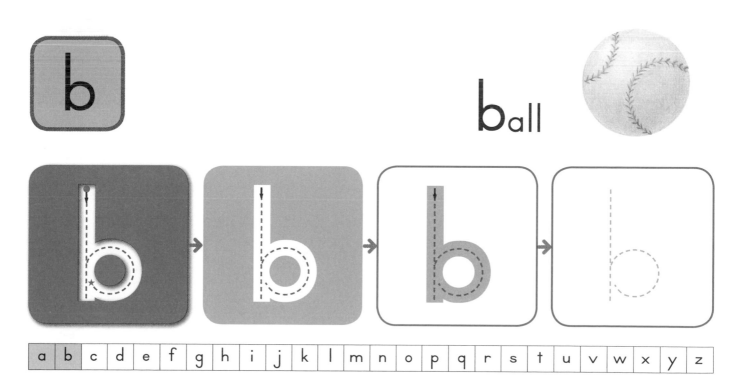

b
ball

| a | b | c | d | e | f | g | h | i | j | k | l | m | n | o | p | q | r | s | t | u | v | w | x | y | z |

Writing **c** and **d**

■ Trace the letters.

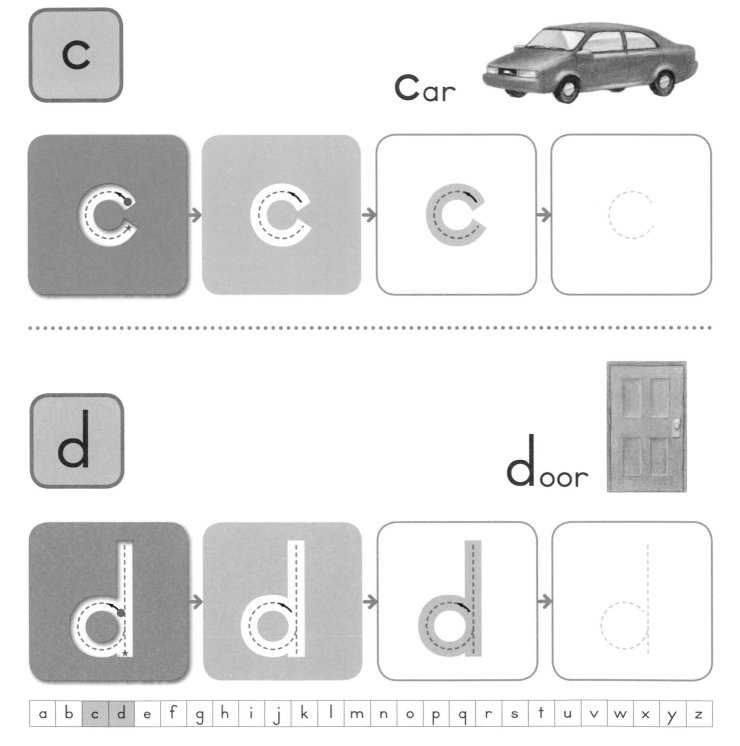

Car

door

Lowercase Letters
Writing **e** and **f**

■ Trace the letters.

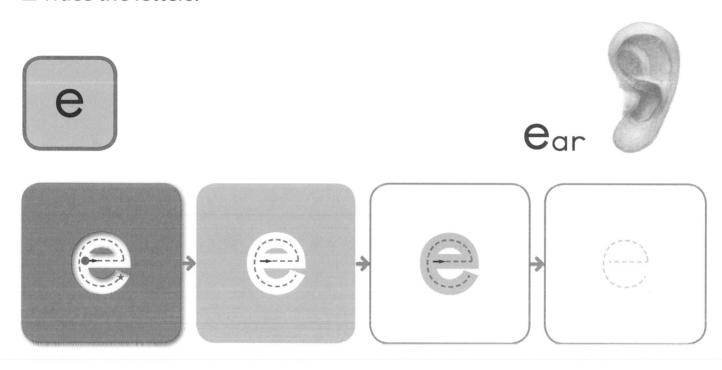

e

e**ar**

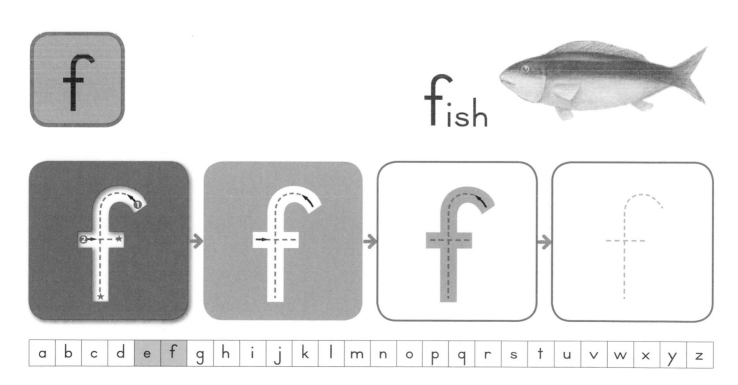

f

f**ish**

| a | b | c | d | e | f | g | h | i | j | k | l | m | n | o | p | q | r | s | t | u | v | w | x | y | z |

Writing **g** and **h**

■ Trace the letters.

girl

hand

| a | b | c | d | e | f | g | h | i | j | k | l | m | n | o | p | q | r | s | t | u | v | w | x | y | z |

Lowercase Letters
Writing **i** and **j**

Name

....
Date

■ Trace the letters.

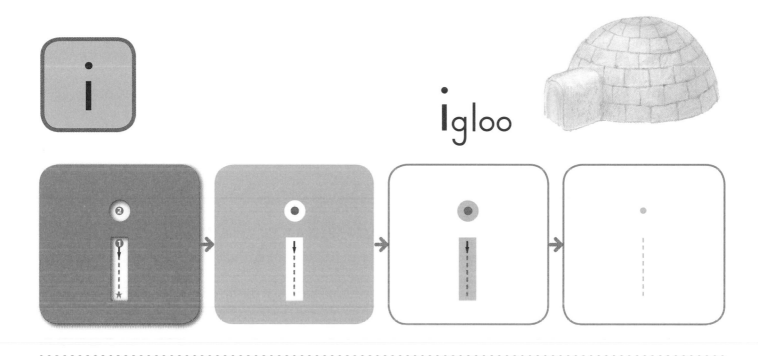

igloo

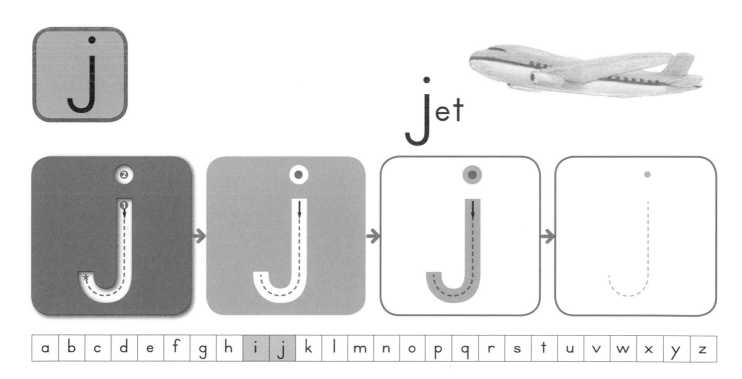

jet

| a | b | c | d | e | f | g | h | i | j | k | l | m | n | o | p | q | r | s | t | u | v | w | x | y | z |

Writing **k** and **l**

■ Trace the letters.

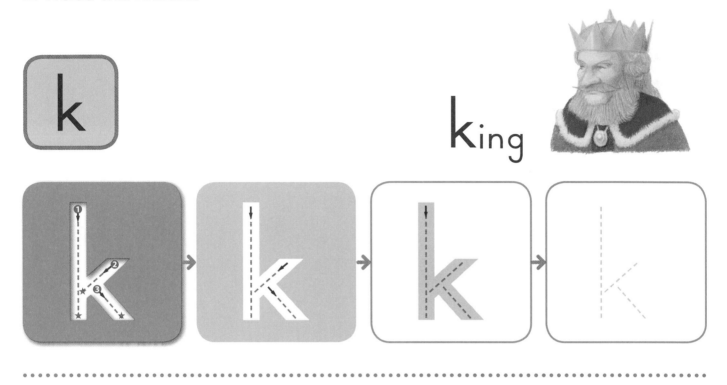

k_{ing}

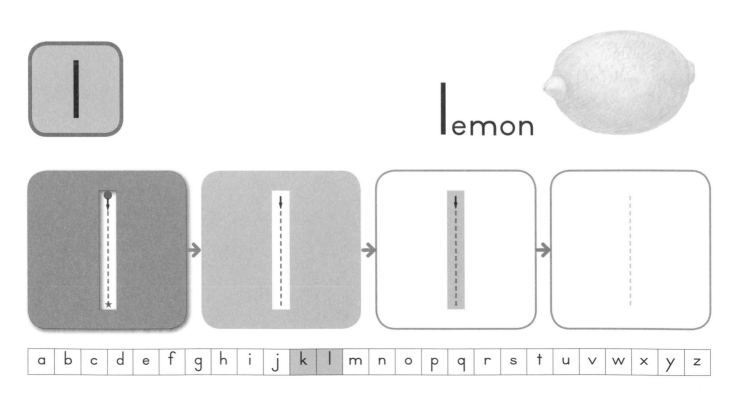

l_{emon}

| a | b | c | d | e | f | g | h | i | j | k | l | m | n | o | p | q | r | s | t | u | v | w | x | y | z |

Lowercase Letters
Writing **m** and **n**

Name

Date

To parents If your child is having difficulty tracing any of these letters, try our other workbooks, such as *My First Book of LOWERCASE LETTERS,* for additional practice.

■ Trace the letters.

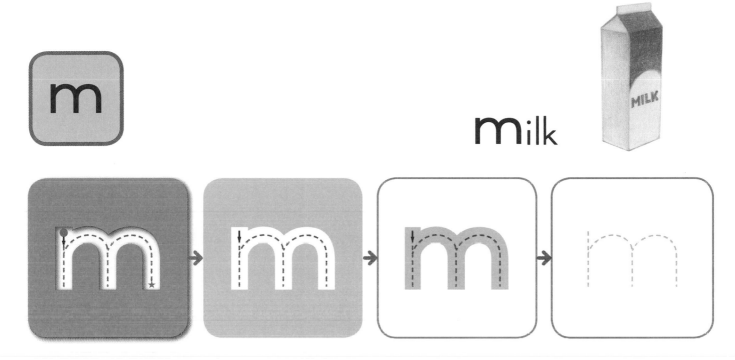

milk

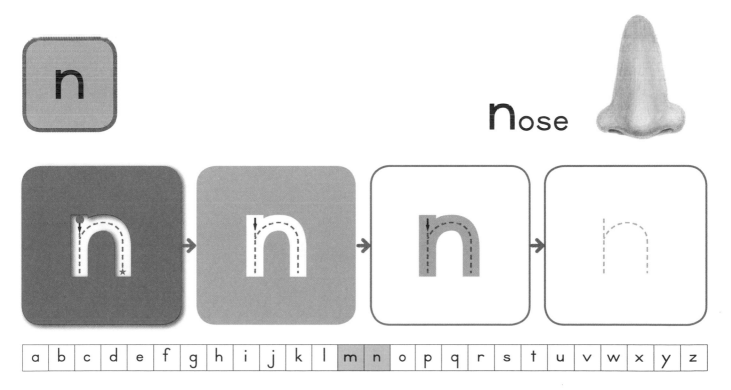

nose

a b c d e f g h i j k l **m** **n** o p q r s t u v w x y z

Writing **o** and **p**

■ Trace the letters.

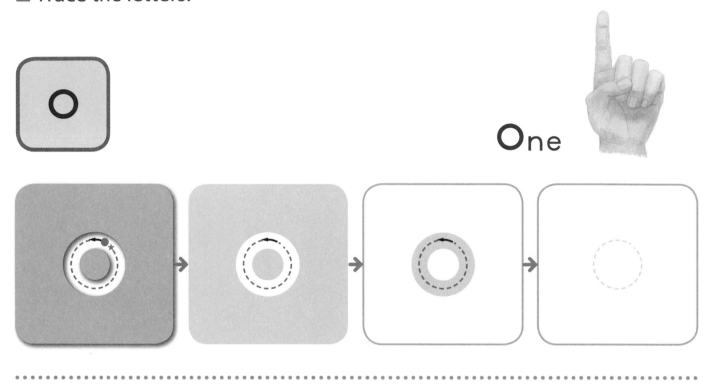

One

Pig

| a | b | c | d | e | f | g | h | i | j | k | l | m | n | o | p | q | r | s | t | u | v | w | x | y | z |

To parents Because of the way these letters are shaped, they are particularly difficult to write. Please praise your child for their hard work.

■ Trace the letters.

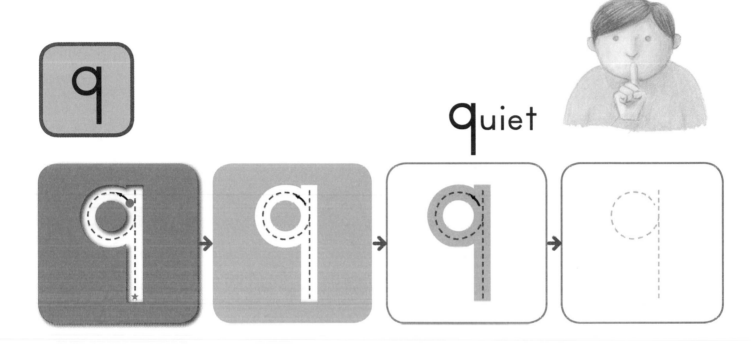

q   quiet

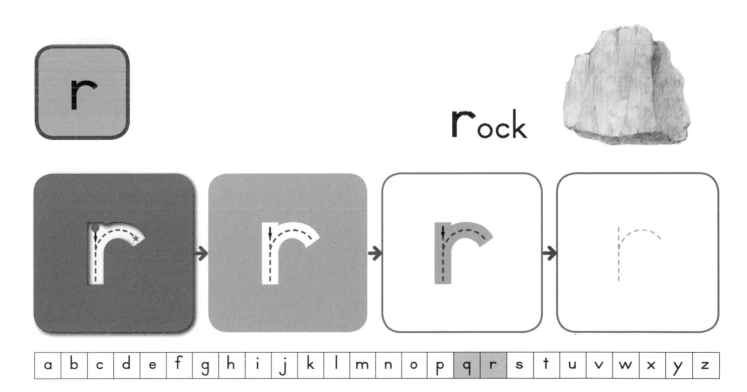

r   rock

| a | b | c | d | e | f | g | h | i | j | k | l | m | n | o | p | q | r | s | t | u | v | w | x | y | z |

43

Writing **s** and **t**

■ Trace the letters.

Sand

tree

| a | b | c | d | e | f | g | h | i | j | k | l | m | n | o | p | q | r | s | t | u | v | w | x | y | z |

Lowercase Letters
Writing **u** and **v**

Name

Date

■ Trace the letters.

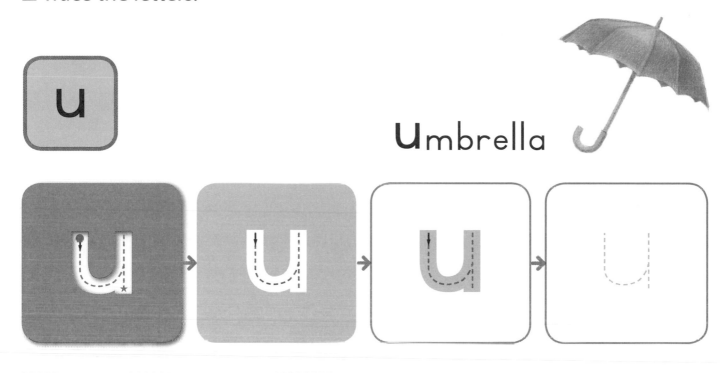

Umbrella

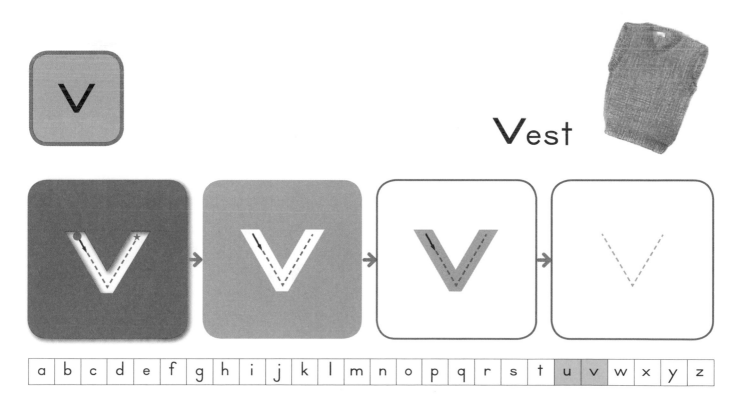

Vest

| a | b | c | d | e | f | g | h | i | j | k | l | m | n | o | p | q | r | s | t | u | v | w | x | y | z |

Writing **w** and **x**

■ Trace the letters.

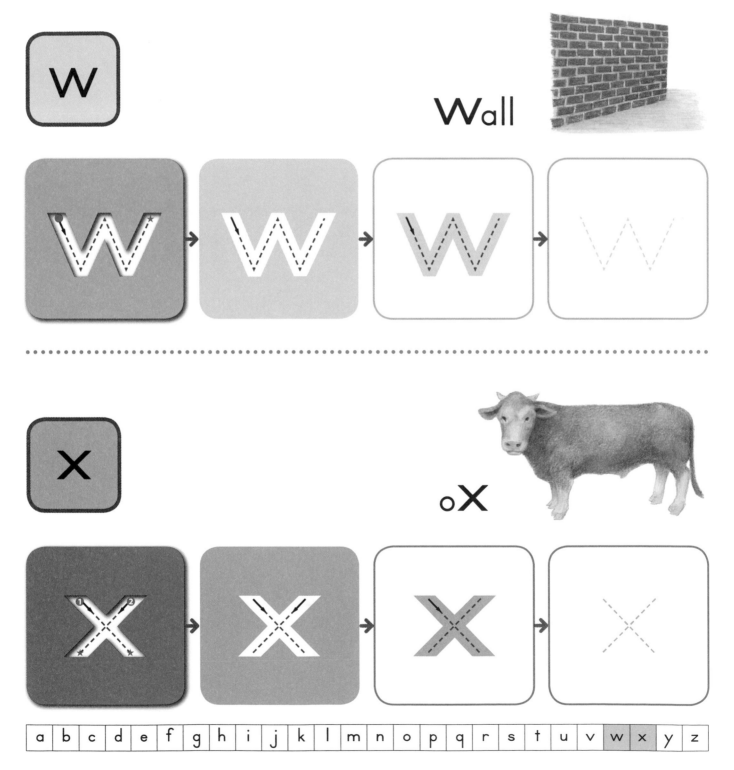

Wall

oX

| a | b | c | d | e | f | g | h | i | j | k | l | m | n | o | p | q | r | s | t | u | v | w | x | y | z |

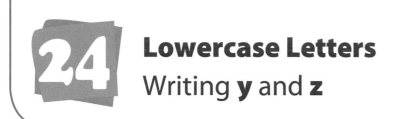

■ Trace the letters.

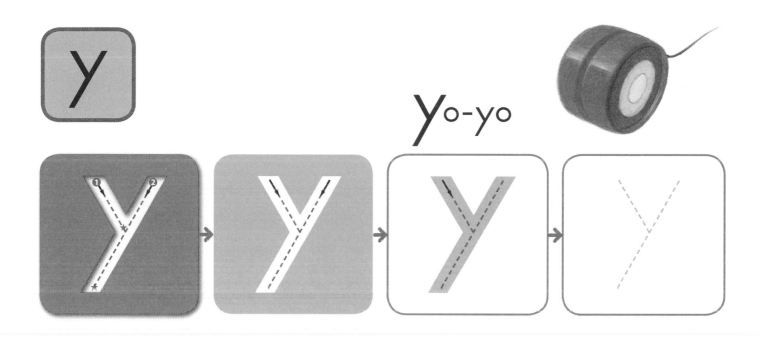

Yo-yo

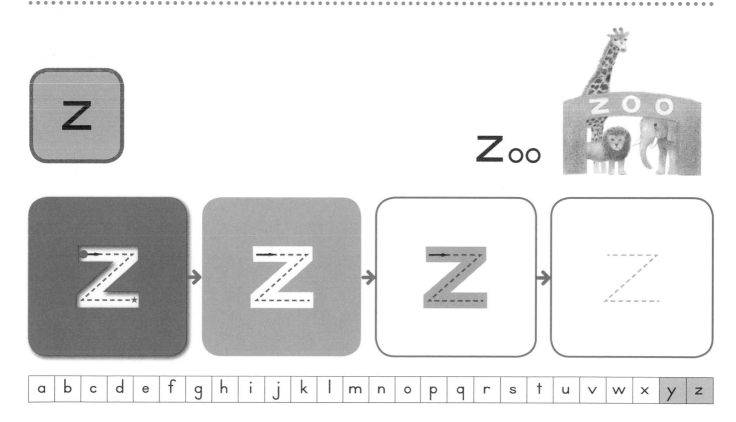

Zoo

| a | b | c | d | e | f | g | h | i | j | k | l | m | n | o | p | q | r | s | t | u | v | w | x | y | z |

Review **a** to **z**

■ Trace the letters in the table below.

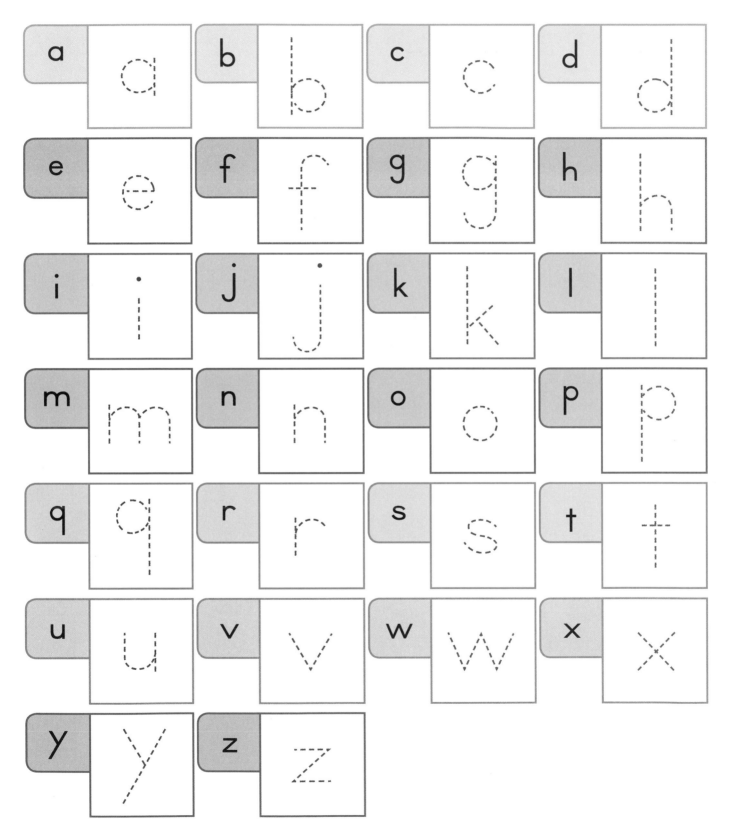

Writing Words
'a' Sound

Name

Date

To parents On the following pages, your child will practice tracing words in rhyming pairs. By repeating rhyming words with the short "a" vowel sound, your child will gain an awareness of the connection between letters and the sounds they represent.

■ Say each letter aloud as you trace it. Then try to say the word aloud. Pay special attention to the letters in color.

■ Say each letter aloud as you trace it. Then try to say the word aloud. Pay special attention to the letters in color.

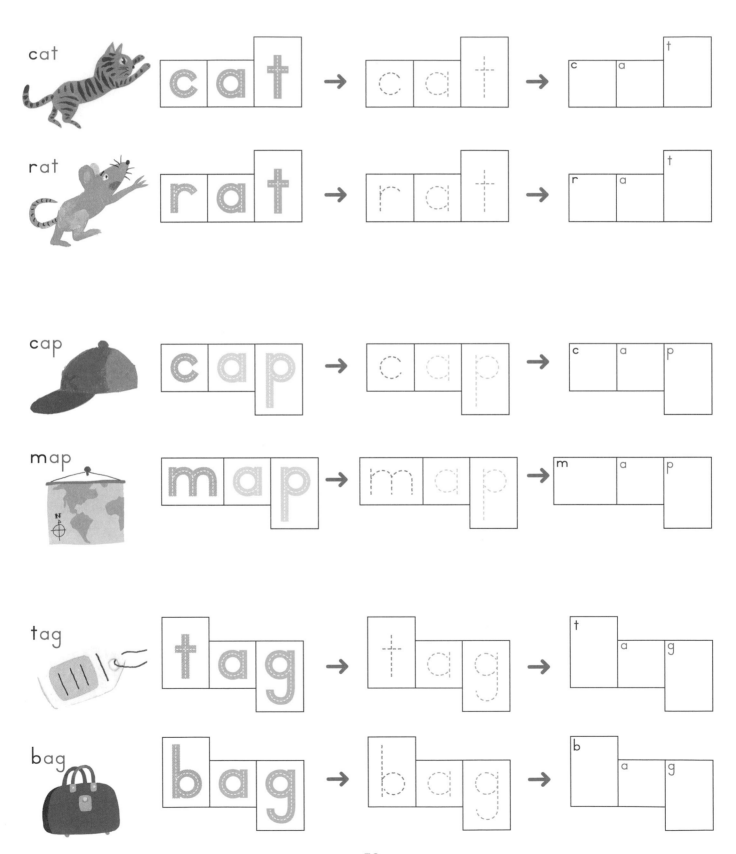

cat

rat

cap

map

tag

bag

Writing Words
'e' Sound

Name

Date

To parents Please help your child to say the sound of the individual letters as he or she traces them. Children should not be forced to blend the letters or sound out the words until they are ready. Try to allow your child to demonstrate their skills naturally, so that they develop positive feelings about learning independently.

■ Say each letter aloud as you trace it. Then try to say the word aloud. Pay special attention to the letters in color.

■ Say each letter aloud as you trace it. Then try to say the word aloud.
Pay special attention to the letters in color.

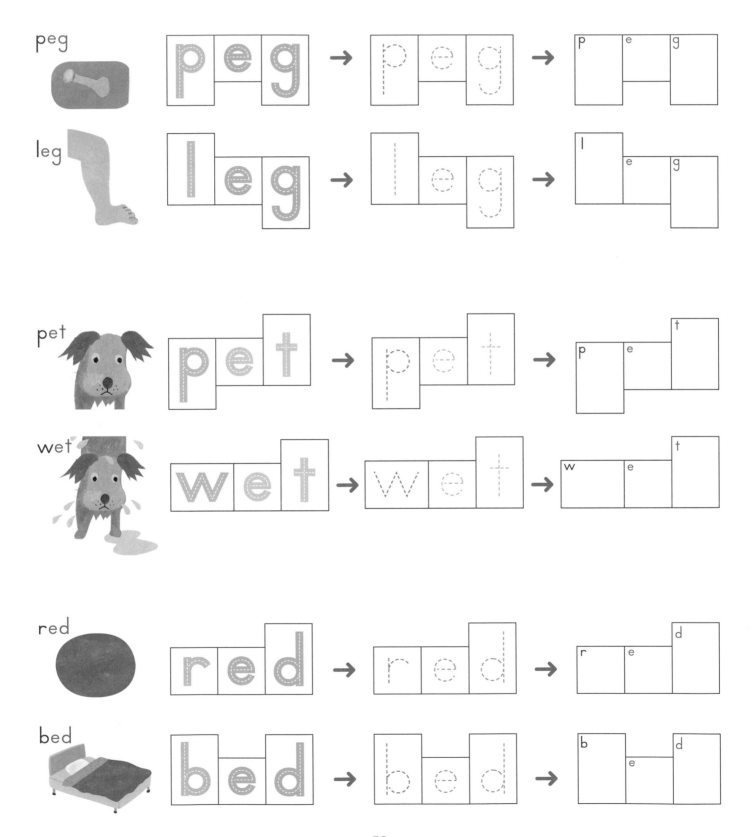

peg

leg

pet

wet

red

bed

Writing Words
'i' Sound

Name

....

Date

To parents If your child is having trouble completing the exercises on these pages, try our other workbooks, such as *My Book of RHYMING WORDS* or *My Book of RHYMING WORDS & PHRASES*, for more practice.

■ Say each letter aloud as you trace it. Then try to say the word aloud. Pay special attention to the letters in color.

tin

pin

pig

lip

hip

dig

■ Say each letter aloud as you trace it. Then try to say the word aloud.
  Pay special attention to the letters in color.

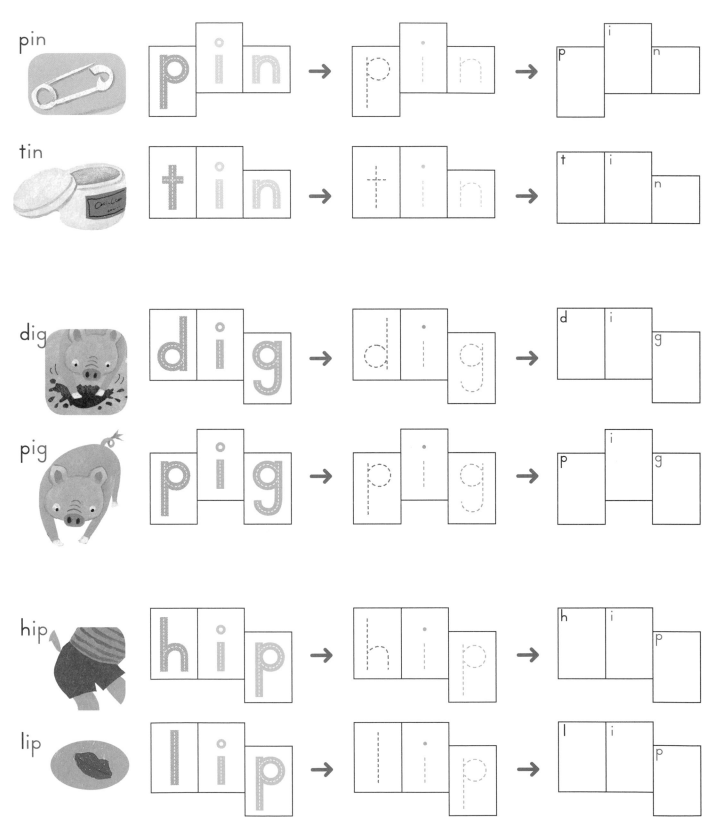

pin

tin

dig

pig

hip

lip

Writing Words
'o' Sound

Name

Date

To parents Writing words can be a difficult exercise for young children. Be sure to give your child plenty of encouragement and praise for their hard work.

■ Say each letter aloud as you trace it. Then try to say the word aloud. Pay special attention to the letters in color.

top

hop

dog

log

hot

pot

■ Say each letter aloud as you trace it. Then try to say the word aloud. Pay special attention to the letters in color.

hop

top

dog

log

hot

pot

■ Say each letter aloud as you trace it. Then try to say the word aloud. Pay special attention to the letters in color.

■ Say each letter aloud as you trace it. Then try to say the word aloud.
Pay special attention to the letters in color.

run

sun

cup

pup

bug

rug

■ Write the uppercase letters in the table below.

A	B	C	D	E	F
G	H	I	J	K	L
M	N	O	P	Q	R
S	T	U	V	W	X
Y	Z				

Review

Lowercase Letters

■ Write the lowercase letters in the table below.

Review
Rhyming Words

To parents Do not be concerned with your child's results on these review pages. Typically, your child will be working on these concepts in kindergarten and this practice will serve as good preparation for that work. Remember to encourage your child for his or her hard work.

■ Write the words below. Use the pictures and letters as hints.

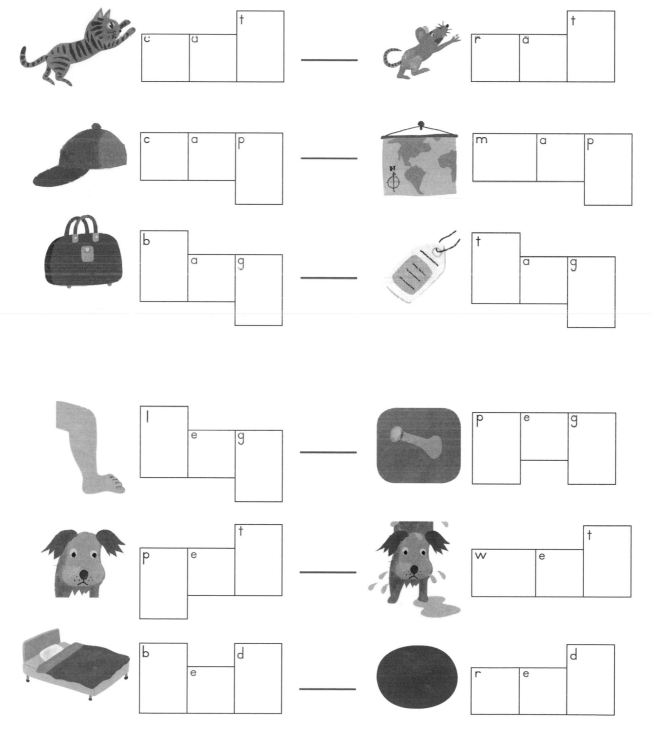

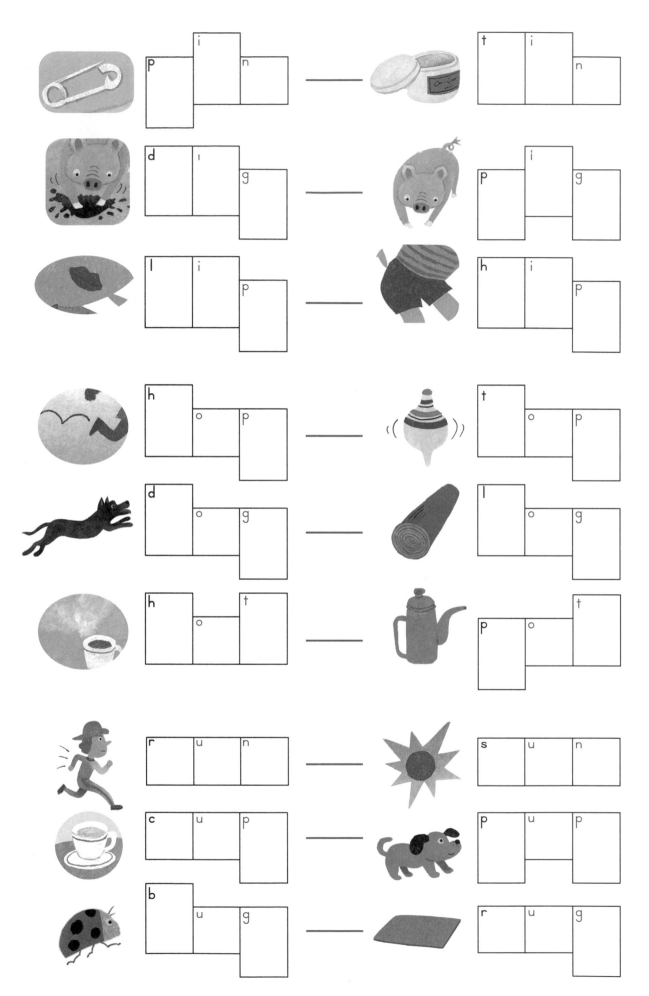

KUMON

Certificate of Achievement

is hereby congratulated on completing

Are You Ready for Kindergarten? Verbal Skills

Presented on _____ , 20___

_____

Parent or Guardian